HRH Princess Dillys Wright

The Rt Hon. Andrew Medhurst

HRH Prince John Richard Wright

HRH Princess Deana Wright

Innovative food systems

1st published in 2020

I0696076

"Climate change is one of the most pressing issues facing our world today, and our food systems have a critical role to play in addressing it. Sustainable food systems can reduce greenhouse gas emissions, improve soil health, and protect biodiversity, while also providing nutritious food for all. By prioritizing sustainability in our food systems, we can build a healthier, more resilient planet for generations to come."
- Dr. Agnes Kalibata, Special Envoy of the UN Secretary-General for the 2021 Food Systems Summit.

Foreword

Food systems and sustainability are closely intertwined, as the way we produce, distribute, and consume food has significant impacts on the environment, society, and economy. There are many ways in which food systems can support sustainability. Regenerative agriculture is a set of practices that aim to improve soil health, sequester carbon, and promote biodiversity. By adopting these practices, farmers can reduce their environmental impact while also improving the quality and yield of their crops. Food waste is a major contributor to greenhouse gas emissions, as rotting food releases methane, a potent greenhouse gas. By reducing food waste through better storage, distribution, and consumption practices, the world can reduce its carbon footprint and conserve resources. By sourcing food from local, organic, and fair trade producers, we can reduce the environmental impact of transportation, promote biodiversity, and support small-scale farmers. Animal agriculture is a major contributor to greenhouse gas emissions and deforestation. By promoting alternative protein sources, such as plant-based and cultured meat, we can reduce the environmental impact of food production while also providing nutritious and affordable food for all. A circular economy approach to food systems involves reducing waste and reusing resources, such as by composting food scraps and using them to fertilize crops. This approach can reduce greenhouse gas emissions, conserve resources, and promote economic sustainability. Sustainability is essential for the long-term viability of our food systems. By adopting all these sustainable practices and more, we can improve the health of the planet, promote social equity, and ensure access to nutritious and affordable food for all. – HRH Princess Agnes Wright

Table of Contents

Innovative food systems

Innovative food systems refer to new and creative approaches to producing, distributing, and consuming food that are designed to improve sustainability, efficiency, and access. These systems aim to address the challenges facing traditional food systems, such as climate change, food insecurity, and waste. Innovative food systems are new and creative ways of producing, distributing, and consuming food that are more sustainable, efficient, and equitable.

These systems often involve the use of new technologies, practices, and business models to address the challenges of food security, nutrition, and environmental sustainability. New technologies are increasingly being used to transform food systems, from production and processing to distribution and consumption. Some examples of

innovative food systems are included in this book.

Vertical farming

This involves growing crops in vertically stacked layers using artificial

lighting and controlled environmental conditions. This allows for year-

round production in urban areas with limited space and reduces the

need for pesticides and herbicides. This is a method of growing crops

in vertically stacked layers, using artificial lighting and controlled

environments. Vertical farming can produce more food per square foot

than traditional farming, and uses less water and pesticides.

This technology involves growing crops in vertically stacked layers,

using artificial lighting and controlled environments. Vertical farming has been shown to produce more food per square foot than traditional farming, and can be located in urban areas to reduce the distance food needs to travel. Vertical farming technology involves growing crops in stacked layers, using artificial lighting and a controlled environment. This technology has produced more food per square foot than traditional farming, and uses less water and pesticides.

This is a method of growing crops in vertically stacked layers, often in a controlled environment. This technology can increase food production per square foot and reduce water usage and pesticide application. Vertical farming is a method of growing crops in vertically stacked layers, using artificial lighting and controlled environments. This technology allows for year-round production of fresh produce in urban areas, using less water and pesticides than traditional farming.

Vertical food systems are a method of growing crops in vertically stacked layers, using artificial lighting and controlled environments. This method of food production allows for year-round production of fresh produce in urban areas, using less water and pesticides than traditional farming. In a vertical food system, plants are grown in stacked layers, often using hydroponic or aeroponic systems that deliver nutrients directly to the roots of the plants. Artificial lighting is used to simulate sunlight, and environmental factors such as temperature, humidity, and CO2 levels are carefully controlled to optimize plant growth.

Vertical food systems can be in urban areas, close to consumers, reducing the need for long-distance transportation of fresh produce. They can also be designed to operate on a smaller scale than traditional farming, making it easier for small-scale farmers to compete in the marketplace. Vertical food systems offer an exciting opportunity to transform the way we produce and consume food, making our food systems more sustainable, efficient, and resilient. Vertical food systems are a form of urban agriculture that involves growing crops in vertically stacked layers, often using hydroponic or aeroponic systems. This method of food production is becoming increasingly popular in urban areas, where space is limited and traditional agriculture is often impractical. Vertical food systems have several potential benefits including,

Increased food security and providing fresh produce

Vertical food systems can produce fresh produce year-round, regardless of weather or season, improving food security in urban areas. Because vertical farms can be in or near urban areas, they can provide fresh produce to consumers year-round, reducing the need for imported fruits and vegetables.

Reduced environmental impact

Vertical food systems use less water and pesticides than traditional farming, and can be located closer to consumers, reducing the environmental impact of food transportation.

Increased efficiency and maximizing space

Vertical food systems can produce higher yields per square foot than traditional farming, making them more efficient. Vertical farming allows to produce a large amount of food in a relatively small space. This is particularly important in urban areas where space is at a premium.

Increased innovation

Vertical food systems offer opportunities for innovation in agriculture, such as the development of new crop varieties and farming techniques.

Saving resources

Vertical farming uses less water and fewer pesticides than traditional

farming methods. Additionally, because crops are grown indoors, there

is no need for soil, which can reduce the risk of soil-borne diseases and

pests.

Increasing yields

Vertical farming can produce higher yields per unit of land compared

to traditional agriculture. This is because crops can be grown year-

round, and the controlled environment allows for optimal growing

conditions.

Reducing transportation

Vertical farms can be in or near urban areas, reducing the need for

long-distance transportation of fresh produce.

Vertical food systems have the potential to provide a sustainable and

efficient way of producing food in urban areas, while also providing

fresh produce to consumers and reducing the environmental impact of

agriculture. However, the high costs of setting up and maintaining

vertical farms can be a barrier to widespread adoption.

Precision agriculture

Precision agriculture uses data and technology to optimize crop yields while reducing waste and environmental impact. This can include using drones and sensors to monitor soil moisture and nutrient levels and using GPS to guide planting and harvesting equipment.

This is the use of sensors, drones, and other technologies to monitor crop growth and optimize yields. Precision agriculture can reduce the use of water, fertilizer, and pesticides, and improve the efficiency of food production. Precision agriculture uses sensors, drones, and other technologies to monitor crop growth and optimize yields so as to reduce the use of water, fertilizer, and pesticides, and improve the efficiency of food production.

Precision agriculture is a technology-driven approach to farming that involves using data and analytics to optimize crop production and reduce waste. This approach uses a combination of sensors, drones, GPS mapping, and other technologies to collect data on crop growth and soil conditions. The data is then analysed to make informed decisions about irrigation, fertilization, and other inputs that affect crop yields and quality. Precision agriculture can have several benefits for food systems, including,

Reducing waste

By using data to optimize crop inputs, precision agriculture can help reduce the amount of fertilizer and water used on crops, reducing waste and environmental impact.

Improving yields

By providing farmers with real-time information on crop growth and

soil conditions, precision agriculture can help them make more

informed decisions about planting, fertilization, and other factors that

affect crop yields.

Enhancing food safety

Precision agriculture can help farmers identify and manage potential

risks to food safety, such as pesticide residues and contaminants.

Supporting sustainable agriculture

Precision agriculture can help farmers adopt more sustainable farming

practices, such as reduced tillage and cover cropping, which can

improve soil health and reduce erosion.

Increasing profitability

By optimizing crop inputs and reducing waste, precision agriculture

can help farmers increase their profitability and reduce their costs.

Precision agriculture has the potential to transform food systems by

improving the efficiency and sustainability of agriculture, while also

providing farmers with the tools and information they need to make

informed decisions about their crops.

Plant-based proteins

Plant-based proteins are becoming more popular as an alternative to meat, due to concerns about the environmental impact of animal agriculture. Innovative food companies are developing new plant-based products that mimic the taste and texture of meat, such as Beyond Meat and Impossible Foods.

Plant-based proteins are becoming increasingly popular as an alternative to traditional animal-based proteins in food systems. Plant-based proteins can be sourced from a variety of plant-based sources, including legumes, grains, nuts, and seeds, and can be used to make a wide range of food products, including burgers, sausages, milk, cheese, and yogurt. There are several benefits of incorporating plant-based proteins into food systems, including,

Health and addressing health concerns

Plant-based proteins are generally lower in saturated fat and higher in

fibre compared to animal-based proteins, which can help reduce the

risk of chronic diseases such as heart disease, diabetes, and cancer.

Plant-based proteins are often lower in saturated fat and cholesterol

than animal-based proteins, making them a healthier option for

consumers

Sustainability and reducing environmental impact

Plant-based proteins require less land, water, and other resources to

produce compared to animal-based proteins, which can help reduce

the environmental impact of food production. Plant-based proteins

have a much lower environmental impact than animal-based proteins.

For example, producing a pound of beef requires 20 times more land,
20 times more water, and produces 20 times more greenhouse gas
emissions than producing a pound of peas.

Improving Food security

Plant-based proteins can be produced more efficiently and at a lower
cost than animal-based proteins, which can help increase access to
protein-rich foods for people who may not be able to afford meat.
Plant-based proteins can be produced more efficiently than animal-
based proteins, making them a more sustainable and cost-effective
source of protein. This can help improve food security, particularly in
developing countries where access to animal protein is limited.

Supporting Innovation

The rise of plant-based proteins has spurred innovation in the food industry, with companies developing new products and technologies to meet consumer demand. The growing popularity of plant-based proteins has spurred innovation in food systems, with many companies developing new and innovative plant-based products to meet consumer demand.

Animal welfare

The use of plant-based proteins can help reduce the demand for animal-based proteins, which can help reduce the number of animals raised for food and improve animal welfare.

Meeting changing consumer demand

As more consumers adopt plant-based diets, food producers and retailers are responding by offering a wider range of plant-based products, including meat substitutes and dairy alternatives.

Incorporating plant-based proteins into food systems has the potential to provide a range of benefits, including improved health outcomes, reduced environmental impact, increased food security, and improved animal welfare. Plant-based proteins are a growing trend in the food industry, with more and more consumers looking for plant-based alternatives to animal products. Plant-based proteins are derived from a variety of sources, including legumes, grains, and vegetables, and can be used to create a wide range of food products, such as meat substitutes, dairy alternatives, and protein powders.

Alternative protein sources

With the rise of plant-based and cell-based meat alternatives, there is a growing trend towards using alternative protein sources, such as insects and algae. These sources have a lower environmental impact than traditional livestock production and can provide a more sustainable source of protein.

Alternative protein sources refer to a range of non-traditional sources of protein that are being developed to supplement or replace animal-based proteins in the food system. These sources can include insect-based proteins, lab-grown meat, and algae-based proteins, among others. Alternative protein sources refer to any sources of protein that are not derived from traditional animal sources such as meat, dairy, and eggs. There are several alternative protein sources that are becoming increasingly popular in food systems. Alternative protein sources have several potential benefits for food systems, including

Reducing environmental impact

Many alternative protein sources have a much lower environmental impact than traditional animal-based proteins. For example, insects require less land, water, and feed than traditional livestock, and produce fewer greenhouse gas emissions. Alternative protein sources have a much lower environmental impact than traditional animal sources. For example, producing a pound of beef requires 20 times more land, 20 times more water, and produces 20 times more greenhouse gas emissions than producing a pound of peas.

Meeting changing consumer demand

As more consumers adopt plant-based and flexitarian diets, alternative protein sources are emerging to provide a wider range of protein options that are aligned with changing consumer preferences. As more consumers adopt plant-based diets, food producers and retailers are responding by offering a wider range of alternative protein products.

Addressing food security concerns

Alternative protein sources can be produced more efficiently and with less resources than traditional animal-based proteins, which can help address food security concerns, particularly in developing countries. Alternative protein sources can be produced more efficiently than traditional animal sources, making them a more sustainable and cost-effective source of protein. This can help improve food security, particularly in developing countries where access to animal protein is

limited.

Addressing health concerns

Many alternative protein sources are often lower in saturated fat and

cholesterol than traditional animal sources, making them a healthier

option for consumers.

Supporting innovation

The development of alternative protein sources is driving innovation

in the food industry, with companies and researchers exploring new

ways to produce and process proteins. The rise of alternative protein

sources has spurred innovation in the food industry, with companies

developing new products and technologies to meet consumer

demand.

Improving animal welfare

Some alternative protein sources, such as lab-grown meat, have the potential to reduce the need for traditional animal agriculture and improve animal welfare.

While there are still challenges to overcome, such as cost, taste, and regulatory hurdles, alternative protein sources have the potential to transform food systems by providing a more sustainable and diverse source of protein, meeting changing consumer preferences, and promoting innovation in the food industry. Alternative protein sources have the potential to transform food systems by providing a more sustainable, efficient, and ethical source of protein, while also meeting changing consumer demand and promoting innovation in the food industry. There are several alternative protein sources that are becoming increasingly popular in food systems including,

Insects

Insects are a highly nutritious and sustainable source of protein. They require very little space, water, and feed to produce, and emit very few greenhouse gases.

Algae

Algae is a highly nutritious and sustainable source of protein that can be grown in a variety of environments, including saltwater, freshwater, and even wastewater.

Single-cell proteins

Single-cell proteins are produced from microbial sources, such as yeast or bacteria, and can be used as a source of protein in food products.

Cultured meat

Cultured meat is produced by growing muscle cells in a laboratory setting, without the need to raise and slaughter animals. This technology has the potential to provide a more sustainable and ethical source of meat.

Plant-based proteins: Plant-based proteins are derived from a variety of sources, such as legumes, grains, and vegetables, and can be used to create a wide range of food products, such as meat substitutes, dairy alternatives, and protein powders.

Food waste reduction

Innovative food systems are also focusing on reducing food waste throughout the supply chain. This can include using predictive analytics to reduce overproduction, developing new packaging materials that extend shelf life, and redistributing surplus food to those in need.

Innovative food systems are also focused on reducing food waste, which is a major problem globally. This includes initiatives to redistribute surplus food to people in need, and to create new products from food waste, such as compost or biofuels.

Food waste reduction is a critical issue in food systems, as it has significant economic, social, and environmental impacts. According to the United Nations, one-third of all food produced globally is lost or wasted, which amounts to approximately 1.3 billion tons per year.

Food waste reduction is a crucial aspect of sustainable food systems.

The food system encompasses all the activities involved in producing,

processing, transporting, distributing, and consuming food. Reducing

food waste at every stage of the food system is essential for improving

food security, reducing greenhouse gas emissions, and conserving

natural resources. There are several strategies that can be

implemented to reduce food waste in food systems, including,

Prevention

One of the most effective ways to reduce food waste is to prevent it

from occurring in the first place. This can be achieved through better

planning, inventory management, and food handling practices, as well

as by educating consumers on how to reduce food waste in their own

homes.

Recovery

Recovering and redistributing surplus food can help reduce food waste while also addressing food insecurity. This can be done through food banks, food recovery organizations, and other initiatives that connect surplus food with people in need.

Recycling

Food waste can be recycled into compost or other products, such as animal feed, biofuels, or fertilizers. This can help reduce the environmental impact of food waste while also creating new economic opportunities.

Innovation

New technologies and business models can help reduce food waste by improving supply chain efficiency, extending shelf life, and reducing spoilage. For example, smart packaging, data analytics, and predictive technologies can help identify and prevent food waste at different points in the supply chain. Reducing food waste in food systems has several benefits, including,

Economic benefits

Reducing food waste can save businesses money by reducing the cost of purchasing and disposing of surplus food.

Social benefits

Reducing food waste can help address food insecurity by increasing the availability of food for people in need.

Environmental benefits

Reducing food waste can help reduce greenhouse gas emissions,

conserve natural resources, and protect biodiversity.

Ethical benefits

Reducing food waste can help address the ethical issues associated

with wasting food, such as the injustice of throwing away food while

people go hungry.

Reducing food waste in food systems is an important goal that requires

collaboration and innovation across the entire food supply chain, from

farmers and producers to retailers and consumers. Here are some

strategies to reduce food waste in food systems,

Improve supply chain management

Better coordination between farmers, distributors, retailers, and

consumers can reduce waste at each stage of the supply chain.

Accurate forecasting of demand and reducing excess inventory can

prevent food from going unsold and being discarded.

Implement sustainable production practices

Sustainable agriculture practices like regenerative farming and

agroecology can help reduce food waste by improving soil health and

reducing the use of harmful chemicals. These practices can increase

crop yields and reduce food loss due to pests, disease, and weather-

related events.

Adopt innovative packaging and storage technologies

Better packaging and storage solutions can help extend the shelf life

of food products, reducing waste due to spoilage. New technologies

such as smart packaging and controlled atmosphere storage can help

preserve the freshness and quality of food products.

Educate consumers

Consumer education can play a vital role in reducing food waste.

Raising awareness about the impact of food waste on the

environment, the economy, and food security can encourage

consumers to adopt more sustainable food consumption habits, such

as planning meals, storing food properly, and composting.

Promote food donation and recovery

Donating excess food to food banks and other charitable organizations

can help feed people in need and reduce waste. Recovering unsold

food from grocery stores and restaurants and redistributing it to those

in need can also reduce food waste.

In conclusion reducing food waste in food systems requires a multi-

faceted approach that involves collaboration between all stakeholders,

including farmers, processors, retailers, consumers, and policymakers.

Local food systems

Local food systems involve the production and distribution of food within a specific region or community. This can reduce the environmental impact of food transport, support local farmers, and increase access to fresh, healthy food for consumers. New technologies are playing an increasingly important role in transforming the food system, from production to distribution and consumption.

Local food systems refer to the production, distribution, and consumption of food within a specific geographic region. These systems prioritize local food sources and aim to create more sustainable and resilient food systems. Here are some key components of local food systems, Local food systems refer to the production, distribution, and consumption of food within a specific geographic area, often defined by a region, city, or community. These systems aim to strengthen local economies, support small-scale farmers, and

promote sustainable agriculture practices.

Small-scale agriculture

Local food systems prioritize small-scale agriculture over industrial

agriculture. This involves supporting local farmers and ranchers who

use sustainable farming practices and rely on local markets for their

livelihoods.

Direct-to-consumer sales

Local food systems often involve direct-to-consumer sales, such as

farmers' markets, community-supported agriculture (CSA) programs,

and farm-to-table restaurants. These sales channels allow consumers

to purchase fresh, locally grown food directly from the source. Support for local farmers. Local food systems provide opportunities for small-scale farmers to sell their products directly to consumers, cutting out intermediaries and increasing their income. This can help support the local economy and promote sustainable agriculture practices.

Food hubs

Food hubs are central locations where farmers can aggregate and distribute their products to local buyers, such as grocery stores, schools, and hospitals. These hubs help to streamline the distribution process and make local food more accessible to consumers.

Food policy councils and Community involvement

Food policy councils are groups of stakeholders, including farmers, consumers, and policymakers, who work together to create policies that support local food systems. These policies can include zoning laws, land-use regulations, and food procurement policies that prioritize local food sources. Local food systems often involve community members in the production and distribution of food. This can include community-supported agriculture (CSA) programs, farmers markets, and food cooperatives, where consumers have a direct relationship with the farmers who grow their food.

Seasonal eating

Local food systems encourage consumers to eat seasonally and to be more connected to the natural rhythms of their local environment. This can help reduce the environmental impact of food production and increase the variety and nutritional value of the food available.

Food security

Local food systems can help increase food security by promoting access to healthy, locally produced food. This can be especially important in areas where access to fresh food is limited, such as urban food deserts.

Food waste reduction

Local food systems prioritize reducing food waste by shortening the supply chain and creating more efficient distribution systems. This can include composting food waste and creating partnerships with food recovery organizations to ensure that excess food is redistributed to those in need.

Local food systems prioritize sustainability, social equity, and economic vitality. They provide consumers with fresh, healthy, and locally grown food while supporting local farmers and strengthening local economies. Local food systems offer a range of benefits, from supporting local economies to promoting sustainable agriculture practices and increasing food security. However, they also face challenges, such as limited infrastructure, higher prices for consumers, and limited availability of certain foods outside of their growing season.

New Technology

New technologies are playing an increasingly important role in the development of modern food systems. New technologies are playing an increasingly important role in transforming the way we produce, distribute, and consume food. These new technologies are transforming the food system by improving efficiency, reducing waste, and increasing transparency. However, it is important to ensure that these technologies are used responsibly and in ways that promote sustainability and equity in the food system.

New technologies are playing an increasingly important role in food systems, from improving agricultural productivity to enhancing food safety and traceability. These are just a few examples of how new technologies are transforming food systems. As technology continues

to advance, we can expect to see even more innovative solutions to

the challenges facing our food system. Here are some examples of new

technologies that are transforming the food industry. Here are some

examples of how new technologies are being used in food systems,

Blockchain

Blockchain technology can be used to track food from farm to plate, improving traceability and reducing the risk of foodborne illnesses. It also enables consumers to have more information about the origin of their food. Blockchain is a distributed ledger technology that allows for secure, transparent, and immutable record-keeping. In the food system, blockchain can be used to track the movement of food from farm to table, ensuring food safety, quality, and authenticity.

Blockchain technology provides a decentralized and secure way of tracking food products throughout the supply chain, from farm to fork. This technology can help prevent food fraud and increase transparency in the food system. Blockchain technology can also be used to improve the traceability of food products, making it easier to track their journey from farm to table. This can increase transparency and accountability

in the food system.

Blockchain technology can improve the transparency and traceability

of food supply chains, making it easier to track the origin, quality, and

safety of food products. This technology can help track food supply

chains, from farm to table, ensuring greater transparency and

accountability. This can help reduce food fraud, improve food safety,

and increase consumer trust. Blockchain technology enables secure

and transparent tracking of food products from farm to table. This can

improve food safety and traceability, and help consumers make more

informed choices about the products they buy. Blockchain technology

is being used to create more transparent and traceable food supply

chains. This technology can help ensure that food products are sourced ethically and sustainably, and can help prevent food fraud and contamination.

This technology is being used to create more transparency and accountability in the food system. By tracking food products from farm to table using blockchain, consumers can have more confidence in the safety and authenticity of their food. Blockchain technology has the potential to transform the food system by improving traceability, transparency, and accountability. By creating a secure and decentralized database of food transactions, blockchain can help prevent food fraud, reduce food waste, and increase consumer trust in the food system. Here are some ways blockchain technology can be used in food systems,

Traceability

Blockchain can be used to track the movement of food from farm to

fork, providing consumers with information about the origin, quality,

and safety of the food they consume. This can help reduce the risk of

foodborne illnesses and increase consumer confidence in the food

system.

Supply chain management

Blockchain can be used to improve supply chain management by providing real-time information on inventory levels, shipping schedules, and quality control. This can help reduce waste and optimize the distribution of food products.

Food safety

Blockchain can be used to create an immutable record of food safety

inspections, enabling regulators to quickly identify and respond to food

safety issues. This can help prevent outbreaks of foodborne illness and

improve public health.

Sustainability

Blockchain can be used to track the environmental impact of food production and distribution, enabling consumers to make more sustainable food choices. This can help reduce greenhouse gas emissions, conserve natural resources, and promote sustainable agriculture practices.

Food fraud prevention

Blockchain can be used to prevent food fraud by creating a transparent and auditable record of food transactions. This can help prevent the mislabelling of food products, the use of counterfeit ingredients, and other forms of food fraud.

Blockchain technology has the potential to improve the efficiency, transparency, and safety of the food system. However, it is important to ensure that the technology is implemented in a way that protects

consumer privacy and data security, and that it is accessible to all

participants in the food system, including small-scale farmers and

consumers in low-income communities.

Internet of Things (IoT)

IoT technology can be used to monitor crops and livestock, enabling farmers to make more informed decisions about irrigation, fertilization, and disease control. It can also help reduce waste and optimize logistics in the supply chain. IoT is a network of interconnected devices that can communicate and exchange data. In the food system, IoT can be used to monitor food production, storage, and transport, optimising conditions, and reducing waste. New technologies are rapidly transforming food systems, from the way food is produced to the way it is consumed.

The Internet of Things (IoT) refers to a network of connected devices and sensors that can communicate and share data with each other. In the food system, IoT technology can be used to monitor and optimize food production, processing, storage, and distribution. Here are some ways IoT can be used in food systems,

Precision agriculture

IoT sensors can be used to monitor soil moisture levels, temperature, and other environmental factors to optimize crop yields and reduce water and fertilizer usage. IoT can be used to monitor soil moisture, temperature, and nutrient levels, enabling farmers to optimize irrigation, fertilization, and other inputs. This can help increase crop yields, reduce water and fertilizer use, and improve soil health.

Smart food storage and packaging

IoT sensors can be used to monitor the temperature, humidity, and other conditions in food storage facilities, reducing spoilage and food waste. IoT can be used to create smart packaging that can monitor the quality and freshness of food products during storage and transportation. This can help prevent food waste and improve the quality of food products. Smart food storage and packaging involves the use of technology to extend the shelf life of food products, reduce food waste, and improve the safety and quality of food. Here are some examples of smart food storage and packaging:

Active packaging

Active packaging involves the use of materials that can actively interact with the food product to extend its shelf life. For example, oxygen scavengers can remove oxygen from the package to reduce spoilage, and antimicrobial agents can prevent the growth of bacteria and fungi.

Modified atmosphere packaging (MAP)

MAP involves the use of a gas mixture in the package to extend the shelf life of the food product. For example, the use of nitrogen or carbon dioxide can reduce the growth of bacteria and delay spoilage.

Smart sensors

Smart sensors can be embedded in the packaging to monitor the temperature, humidity, and other conditions inside the package. This can help to ensure that the food product is stored at the appropriate conditions and reduce the risk of spoilage.

Time-temperature indicators (TTIs)

TTIs are labels that change colour based on the temperature and time that the food product has been exposed to. This can help consumers and retailers to quickly identify food products that have been exposed to temperatures that could cause spoilage.

Vacuum packaging

Vacuum packaging involves the removal of air from the package to
extend the shelf life of the food product. This can help to reduce
oxidation and prevent the growth of bacteria and fungi.

Smart food storage and packaging can help to reduce food waste,
improve food safety, and extend the shelf life of food products.
However, it is important to ensure that the packaging materials and
technology used are safe, sustainable, and cost-effective.

Real-time inventory management

IoT sensors can be used to track inventory levels and monitor the
movement of food products throughout the supply chain, improving
supply chain efficiency and reducing waste. Real-time inventory

management is a process of monitoring and controlling inventory levels in real-time using technology such as sensors, barcodes, and RFID (radio-frequency identification). It allows businesses to track inventory levels and movements accurately and quickly, enabling them to make better decisions about inventory replenishment, ordering, and pricing. Here are some benefits of real-time inventory management,

Improved inventory accuracy

Real-time inventory management provides accurate and up-to-date information on inventory levels, reducing the risk of stockouts, overstocking, and shrinkage. This can help businesses save money on inventory carrying costs and improve customer satisfaction by ensuring that products are available when customers need them.

Reduced manual labour

Real-time inventory management reduces the need for manual inventory counts, which can be time-consuming and prone to errors. This can save businesses time and money, allowing them to focus on other aspects of their operations

Efficient order fulfilment

Real-time inventory management allows businesses to fulfil orders quickly and accurately by providing real-time information on inventory availability and location. This can help improve order accuracy, reduce shipping times, and increase customer satisfaction.

Better decision-making

Real-time inventory management provides businesses with real-time data on inventory levels, movements, and trends, enabling them to make informed decisions about inventory replenishment, pricing, and promotions. This can help businesses optimize their inventory levels

and increase profitability.

Improved supply chain visibility

Real-time inventory management provides businesses with visibility

into their supply chain, enabling them to track inventory levels and

movements across multiple locations and partners. This can help

businesses identify bottlenecks, reduce lead times, and improve

collaboration with suppliers and partners.

Real-time inventory management can help businesses improve

efficiency, accuracy, and profitability by providing real-time data on

inventory levels and movements. However, it requires investment in technology and infrastructure, as well as a culture of continuous

improvement and data-driven decision-making.

Supply chain management

IoT can be used to track the movement of food products through the

supply chain, providing real-time information on inventory levels,

shipping schedules, and quality control. This can help reduce waste

and optimize the distribution of food products. Supply chain

management is the process of managing the flow of goods, services,

and information from the supplier to the customer. In the food system,

supply chain management is particularly important because of the

perishable nature of food products and the need for timely and

efficient delivery. Here are some key aspects of supply chain

management in the food system,

Traceability

Traceability is the ability to track food products from farm to table. It involves the use of technology, such as barcodes, RFID, and blockchain, to record and track the movement of food products through the supply chain. Traceability helps to ensure the safety and quality of food products and enables businesses to quickly respond to food safety issues.

Inventory management

Inventory management involves the management of inventory levels to ensure that the right products are available at the right time. It involves forecasting demand, managing inventory levels, and optimizing inventory replenishment. Effective inventory management helps to reduce waste and ensure that products are delivered on time.

Logistics

Logistics involves the management of the transportation and storage of food products. It involves the selection of transportation modes, the optimization of routes, and the management of storage facilities. Effective logistics helps to reduce transportation costs, improve delivery times, and ensure that products are stored at the appropriate temperature and humidity.

Quality control

Quality control involves the management of product quality throughout the supply chain. It involves the use of quality standards, such as ISO 22000, to ensure that food products meet the required quality standards. Effective quality control helps to ensure that food products are safe, nutritious, and of high quality.

Collaboration

Collaboration involves the coordination and cooperation between different stakeholders in the food system, including farmers, processors, distributors, retailers, and consumers. Effective collaboration helps to improve efficiency, reduce waste, and ensure that products are delivered on time and to the right location.

Supply chain management is a critical aspect of the food system, and effective management can help to improve efficiency, reduce waste, and ensure the safety and quality of food products.

Food safety monitoring

IoT sensors can be used to monitor the temperature and other conditions of food products during transportation, storage, and distribution, ensuring food safety and reducing the risk of foodborne illness. IoT can be used to monitor the temperature and humidity of food storage facilities, enabling producers and distributors to ensure that food products are stored at the appropriate temperature to prevent spoilage and contamination. IoT sensors can also be used to detect the presence of pathogens and other contaminants in food products, enabling producers to quickly identify and respond to food safety issues.

Smart vending machines and retail stores

IoT sensors can be used to track inventory levels, monitor consumer behaviour, and optimize the layout of retail stores and vending machines, improving the consumer experience, and reducing waste.

Consumer engagement

IoT can be used to create interactive food experiences for consumers,

such as smart kitchens and personalized nutrition apps. This can help

consumers make more informed food choices and improve their

overall health and well-being.

IoT technology has the potential to revolutionize the food system by improving efficiency, reducing waste, and increasing food safety. However, it is important to ensure that the technology is accessible to all participants in the food system, including small-scale farmers and consumers in low-income communities, and that it is implemented in a way that protects consumer privacy and data security.

In conclusion, IoT has the potential to transform the food system by improving efficiency, quality, and safety. However, it is important to ensure that the technology is implemented in a way that protects consumer privacy and data security, and that it is accessible to all participants in the food system, including small-scale farmers and consumers in low-income communities.

Artificial intelligence (AI)

AI technology can be used to analyse data from sensors, cameras, and other sources to optimize crop yields, improve food safety, and reduce waste. AI is the simulation of human intelligence processes by machines, including learning, reasoning, and self-correction. In the food system, AI can be used to optimize crop yields, predict weather patterns, and analyse food safety data. AI technology can be used to analyse large amounts of data on food production and consumption to identify trends and patterns.

This technology can be used to predict food demand, optimize supply chains, and reduce food waste. AI can be used to analyse data on food production, distribution, and consumption to identify trends and patterns, which can help to optimize the food system and improve decision-making. AI can be used in various ways in food systems, such as predicting food demand, optimizing supply chains, and improving crop yields. AI can also help reduce food waste by predicting expiration dates and optimizing food storage.

 AI is being used to improve everything from crop selection to food processing and packaging. For example, AI algorithms can analyse food quality and freshness in real-time, and make decisions about how to package and transport the product. New technologies are helping to create more efficient, sustainable, and resilient food systems that can meet the needs of a growing global population. However, it is important to ensure that these technologies are used in a responsible and ethical way, and that they benefit all members of society. This technology is being used to improve food safety by predicting and preventing foodborne illness outbreaks. AI can also be used to optimize food production, reduce waste, and improve logistics and

distribution.

Artificial intelligence (AI) is increasingly being used in food systems to

improve efficiency, reduce waste, and increase food safety. Here are

some examples of AI in food systems,

Predictive analytics

AI can be used to analyse data on crop yields, weather patterns, and

market trends to predict when and where crops will be most

successful. This can help farmers to make informed decisions about

planting, harvesting, and marketing their crops.

Quality control

AI can be used to inspect food products for defects, such as bruises,

discoloration, and foreign objects. This can help to ensure that only

high-quality products are shipped to customers.

Food safety

 AI can be used to monitor food products for contamination, such as

pathogens or chemical residues, and to identify the source of any

contamination that does occur. This can help to improve food safety

and prevent outbreaks of foodborne illness.

Supply chain management

 AI can be used to track food products as they move through the supply

chain, from farm to table. This can help to improve transparency,

reduce waste, and ensure that products are delivered to customers on

time and in good condition.

Personalized nutrition

AI can be used to analyse data on individual health and dietary preferences to provide personalized nutrition recommendations. This can help to improve health outcomes and reduce the risk of chronic diseases.

AI has the potential to transform food systems by improving efficiency, reducing waste, and increasing food safety. However, it is important to ensure that these technologies are used responsibly and in a way that supports the well-being of workers and the environment.

3D printing

 3D printing can be used to create customized foods and to produce food with specific textures and nutritional profiles. It can also reduce waste by producing food on demand. 3D printing is the process of creating three-dimensional objects by depositing layers of material. In the food system, 3D printing can be used to create customized, nutrient-rich meals for individuals with specific dietary needs. 3D printing technology can be used to create customized foods with precise shapes, textures, and nutritional profiles. This technology can be used to produce food in space or in other remote locations where fresh food is not readily available.

3D printing can be used to create customized food products, such as personalized nutrition bars or pills, which can be tailored to an individual's specific nutritional needs. 3D printing technology can be used to produce customized food products with specific nutritional profiles, textures, and flavours. This technology can also reduce food waste by producing food in precise quantities. This technology allows for the creation of complex food shapes and textures using a variety of ingredients.

This can lead to the creation of new food products and experiences, and may be used in personalized nutrition and medical diets. 3D printing is being used to create new and innovative food products, such as personalized nutrition bars and edible sculptures. This technology can also reduce food waste by allowing chefs to create precise portions of food. 3D printing technology is being used to create new food products, such as customized chocolates, pastries, and pizza. 3D printing can also be used to create food with unique textures and shapes, which could help make food more appealing to consumers.

This technology is being used to create new food products, such as personalized nutrition bars, chocolate, and even entire meals. 3D printing can also be used to create intricate shapes and designs that would be difficult to achieve through traditional food manufacturing methods. 3D printing can also be used to create custom-designed food products, such as personalised nutritional supplements or unique shapes and textures of food. This technology has the potential to reduce food waste, as well as to create new and innovative food products.

3D printing is a technology that allows the creation of three-dimensional objects by adding material layer by layer based on a digital model. In recent years, 3D printing has been applied to the food industry, opening new opportunities for customization, creativity, and innovation in food production. Here are some potential applications of

3D printing in food systems,

Customisation

3D printing can be used to create personalized food products based

on individual dietary requirements, preferences, and tastes. For

example, 3D printing can be used to create customized shapes,

textures, and flavours.

Nutrient customisation

3D printing can be used to create food products that are customized to

meet the specific nutrient needs of individuals. For example, 3D

printers can be used to create food products that are high in protein,

vitamins, or other nutrients.

Innovation

3D printing can be used to create novel food products that are difficult or impossible to produce using traditional manufacturing methods. For example, 3D printing can be used to create complex geometries, such as intricate lattice structures, that would be difficult to create using traditional methods.

Waste reduction

3D printing can be used to reduce food waste by allowing for precise control over the amount of material used in production. For example, 3D printing can be used to create thin and lightweight structures that use less material than traditional manufacturing methods. 3D printing can help to reduce food waste by allowing for the creation of food products with precise measurements and quantities. This can help to reduce the overproduction of food products and the subsequent waste that is often associated with traditional food production methods.

Supply chain efficiency

3D printing can be used to create food products on demand, reducing the need for large-scale production and storage facilities. This can help to reduce transportation costs, minimize food spoilage, and improve supply chain efficiency.

Food safety

3D printing can be used to create food products in a controlled and sterile environment, reducing the risk of contamination and foodborne illness. Additionally, 3D printing can be used to create food products that are easier to digest or that have specific nutritional properties.

Novel food products

3D printing can be used to create new food products that are not possible with traditional food production methods. For example, 3D printing can be used to create food products with unique textures and

shapes, such as edible flowers or intricate sugar sculptures.

Efficiency

3D printing can help to improve the efficiency of food production by

reducing the time and labour required to produce food products. This

can help to increase production volumes and reduce costs.

While 3D printing is a promising technology for the food industry, there

are also challenges that need to be addressed, such as cost, scalability,

and regulatory issues. Nonetheless, 3D printing has the potential to

transform the food industry and provide new opportunities for

innovation and creativity. 3D printing in food systems has great

potential, yet there are still challenges to overcome, including the development of safe and sustainable printing materials and the need

for further research on the nutritional value of 3D printed food

products.

Gene editing

Gene editing technologies like CRISPR can be used to create crops that are more resilient to climate change, require less water and fertilizer, and have longer shelf lives. It can also be used to create plant-based meat alternatives with better taste and texture. Gene editing is the process of making precise changes to the DNA of an organism. In the food system, gene editing can be used to create crops that are more resistant to pests and diseases, and that require fewer resources to grow. Gene editing technology can be used to develop crops that are more resistant to pests and diseases or have a longer shelf life.

This technology can help increase yields and reduce the use of pesticides and other chemicals in food production. Gene editing technologies like CRISPR are being used to develop crops that are more resistant to pests and diseases, and that can thrive in different climates. This can increase food security and resilience in the face of climate change.

Gene editing technologies like CRISPR can be used to develop crops that are more resistant to pests and diseases, and that can thrive in different environmental conditions. This can improve the sustainability and resilience of food production. Gene editing technologies such as CRISPR/Cas9 are being used to create crops with improved traits such as disease resistance, drought tolerance, and higher yields. This can help address challenges such as food insecurity and climate change.

Gene editing is a powerful technology that can be used to modify the DNA of organisms, including plants and animals, to improve their characteristics or traits. In food systems, gene editing has the potential to create crops and livestock that are more resilient, nutritious, and sustainable. Here are some potential applications of gene editing in food systems,

Crop improvement

Gene editing can be used to improve the traits of crops, such as their yield, nutritional content, and resistance to pests and diseases. For example, gene editing can be used to create crops that are more drought-resistant or that have a longer shelf life.

Livestock improvement

Gene editing can be used to improve the traits of livestock, such as their growth rate, disease resistance, and meat quality. For example, gene editing can be used to create livestock that are resistant to specific diseases or that produce leaner meat.

Reduced environmental impact

Gene editing can be used to create crops and livestock that are more

sustainable and have a reduced environmental impact. For example,

gene editing can be used to create crops that require fewer inputs,

such as water or fertilizer, or that have a reduced carbon footprint.

Reduced food waste

Gene editing can be used to create crops that have a longer shelf life

or that are less prone to spoilage, which can help to reduce food waste.

While gene editing has great potential in food systems, there are also

ethical and safety considerations that need to be considered. The long-

term effects of gene editing on the environment and human health are

not yet fully understood, and there is a need for careful regulation and

oversight of gene editing in food systems.

Mobile applications

These apps can help consumers make more informed decisions about their food choices, such as tracking nutritional information, identifying food allergies, and sourcing local and sustainable food options. New technologies are helping to make the food system more efficient, sustainable, and safe. However, it is important to consider the potential social and environmental impacts of these technologies, and ensure that they are used in a responsible and equitable manner.

Mobile applications have become increasingly popular in the food industry, offering a range of services and benefits for both consumers and businesses. Here are some examples of mobile applications in food systems,

Food delivery apps

Food delivery apps have become very popular in recent years, allowing consumers to order food from their favorite restaurants and have it delivered to their doorstep. Popular examples include Uber Eats, Grubhub, DoorDash, and Postmates.

Recipe apps

Recipe apps provide users with access to a variety of recipes, often with step-by-step instructions and photos. Some popular recipe apps include Yummly, Allrecipes, and Tasty.

Nutrition apps

Nutrition apps can help users track their daily intake of calories, nutrients, and other dietary factors. Popular examples include MyFitnessPal and Lose It!.

Food waste reduction apps

Food waste reduction apps can help users reduce food waste by tracking expiration dates, creating grocery lists, and finding recipes that use up leftover ingredients. Popular examples include Too Good To Go, Olio, and NoWaste.

Restaurant and review apps

Restaurant and review apps allow users to search for restaurants and read reviews from other users. Popular examples include Yelp and TripAdvisor.

Food safety apps

Food safety apps can help users ensure that the food they eat is safe and healthy. For example, the USDA's FoodKeeper app provides information on how to store and handle different types of food.

Mobile applications have the potential to improve efficiency, convenience, and accessibility in food systems. However, it is important to ensure that these applications are designed and used in a responsible and ethical manner, considering issues such as data privacy, food safety, and sustainability.

Food safety technology

New technologies are being developed to improve food safety, such as

sensors that can detect foodborne pathogens and smart packaging

that can alert consumers when food has spoiled. New technologies are

playing an increasingly important role in transforming food systems

and making them more sustainable, efficient, and resilient. Food safety

technology is an essential part of modern food systems. Here are some

examples of food safety technology that are commonly used in the

food industry,

Food testing and analysis

Food testing and analysis involves the use of laboratory techniques to

identify and quantify contaminants, such as bacteria, viruses, toxins,

and allergens, in food. Examples of food testing technologies include polymerase chain reaction (PCR), enzyme-linked immunosorbent assay

(ELISA), and mass spectrometry.

Traceability and labelling

Traceability and labelling systems allow food products to be tracked

and identified throughout the supply chain, from farm to table. These

systems can help to prevent foodborne illnesses and ensure that food

products meet regulatory requirements. Examples of traceability and

labelling technologies include barcodes, RFID tags, and blockchain.

Food preservation and processing

Food preservation and processing technologies can help to prevent the

growth of harmful bacteria and increase the shelf life of food products.

Examples of food preservation and processing technologies include

pasteurization, canning, freezing, and irradiation.

Food packaging

Food packaging plays an important role in protecting food products

from contamination and maintaining their quality and freshness.

Innovative food packaging technologies, such as modified atmosphere

packaging and active packaging, can help to extend the shelf life of

food products and improve their safety.

Food safety management systems

Food safety management systems are comprehensive systems that

help food businesses to identify, prevent, and manage food safety risks.

Examples of food safety management systems include Hazard Analysis

and Critical Control Points (HACCP), Good Manufacturing Practices

(GMPs), and the Global Food Safety Initiative (GFSI) standards.

By using food safety technology in food systems, businesses can help

to ensure that their products are safe, healthy, and of high quality.

However, it is important to keep in mind that food safety technology

should be used in conjunction with other measures, such as proper

hygiene and sanitation practices, to ensure the safety of the food

supply.

Cellular agriculture

Cellular agriculture involves growing animal products, such as meat

and dairy, from animal cells rather than from live animals. This

technology has the potential to reduce the environmental impact of

animal agriculture, while also addressing concerns around animal

welfare and food safety. Cellular agriculture, also known as cultured or

lab-grown meat, is an emerging technology in the food industry that involves growing animal cells in a lab to create meat products. Here are

some key points about cellular agriculture,

How it works

Cellular agriculture involves taking a small sample of animal cells and

using them to grow meat tissue in a lab setting. The meat tissue can

then be harvested, processed, and packaged like traditional meat

products.

Benefits

 Cellular agriculture has the potential to reduce the environmental

impact of meat production by using fewer resources and generating

less waste. It can also address animal welfare concerns by reducing the

need for livestock farming.

Challenges

The technology is still in its early stages and faces challenges such as

scaling up production to meet demand and reducing the cost of

production.

Regulatory framework

The regulatory framework for cellular agriculture is still being

developed, with some countries already allowing the sale of cultured

meat products, while others are still in the process of establishing

regulations.

Consumer acceptance

 Consumer acceptance of cultured meat products is still uncertain,

with some consumers expressing concerns about the safety and taste

of the products.

Cellular agriculture has the potential to revolutionize the way we

produce and consume meat, and it will be interesting to see how this

technology develops in the coming years.

Robotics

Robotics technology can be used to automate tasks like planting, harvesting, and packaging, reducing labour costs and increasing efficiency. Robotics and automation are being used in food processing and packaging to increase efficiency and reduce the need for human labour. For example, robots can be used to pick and pack fruits and vegetables, reducing the need for manual labour. Robotics can be used in various stages of food production, from planting and harvesting to processing and packaging. Robots can perform tasks more efficiently than humans and reduce the need for manual labour.

Robotics technology is becoming increasingly popular in the food industry to automate various processes and increase efficiency. Here are some examples of robotics in food systems:

Harvesting and sorting

Robots can be used to harvest crops, such as lettuce and strawberries, and sort them according to size, shape, and quality.

Food processing and packaging

Robots can be used to cut, slice, and package food products, such as fruits, vegetables, and meat. This can help to increase productivity and reduce the risk of contamination.

Quality control

Robots can be used to inspect food products for defects, such as bruises, discoloration, and foreign objects. This can help to ensure that only high-quality products are shipped to customers.

Inventory management

Robots can be used to manage inventory in warehouses and distribution centres. They can be programmed to track the location and quantity of food products, and retrieve them as needed for shipping.

Food service

Robots can be used in food service settings, such as restaurants and cafes, to take orders, prepare food, and deliver it to customers.

The use of robotics technology in food systems has the potential to increase efficiency, reduce labour costs, and improve safety and quality. However, it is important to ensure that these technologies are used responsibly and in a way that supports the well-being of workers and the environment.

Precision agriculture

Precision agriculture uses a range of technologies, including sensors, drones, and GPS, to monitor crop growth and optimize yields. This technology can reduce the use of water, fertilizer, and pesticides, and improve the efficiency of food production. As mentioned earlier, precision agriculture involves the use of sensors, drones, and other technologies to monitor crop growth and optimize yields. This can reduce the use of water, fertilizer, and pesticides, and improve the efficiency of food production. This technology involves using sensors, drones, and other tools to collect data on soil conditions, weather patterns, and crop growth.

This information can be used to optimize crop yields, reduce water and fertilizer use, and improve overall efficiency. For example, farmers can use sensors to monitor soil moisture levels, plant health, and weather conditions, and adjust irrigation and fertilization accordingly. This technology involves using sensors, drones, and other advanced tools to collect data about crop growth, soil health, and weather conditions. This data is used to optimize crop yields, reduce waste, and minimize the use of water, fertilizer, and pesticides. This technology involves the use of other devices to monitor crop growth and optimize yields. This can help reduce water usage, fertilizer, and pesticide applications, and improve overall efficiency. Precision agriculture involves the use of other technologies to collect data on crops, weather conditions, and soil quality. This data can be used to optimize planting, irrigation, and fertilizer use, reducing waste, and increasing yields.

Precision agriculture is an approach to farming that involves the use of technology to optimize crop yields, reduce waste, and improve resource efficiency. Here are some key aspects of precision agriculture

in food systems,

Data collection

Precision agriculture relies on the collection and analysis of data from

a variety of sources, including sensors, drones, satellites, and weather

stations. This data can be used to monitor soil conditions, crop growth,

and weather patterns, among other factors.

Decision-making

The data collected through precision agriculture can be used to make

informed decisions about when to plant, irrigate, fertilize, and harvest

crops. This can help to optimize yields and reduce waste.

Resource efficiency

 Precision agriculture can help to reduce the amount of water, fertilizer, and pesticides needed to grow crops, by targeting these inputs to where they are most needed. This can help to reduce environmental impacts and lower costs.

Automation

Precision agriculture often involves the use of automated machinery, such as drones, tractors, and irrigation systems, to perform tasks more efficiently and accurately than would be possible with manual labour.

Crop variability

Precision agriculture considers the variability of crop growth within a field, and tailors management practices to specific areas of the field based on their unique characteristics.

Precision agriculture has the potential to increase yields, reduce waste, and improve resource efficiency in food systems. However, it requires significant investment in technology and data analysis, and may not be suitable for all types of farming operations.

These are just a few examples of how new technologies are being integrated into the food system to improve efficiency, reduce waste, and create more sustainable and equitable food systems. As technology continues to evolve, it will likely play an increasingly important role in transforming the food system. new technologies are providing exciting opportunities to transform food systems and address some of the key challenges facing the global food system, including climate change, food security, and nutrition.

In conclusion, new technologies are revolutionizing the food system by

improving efficiency, reducing waste, and enhancing sustainability.

However, it's important to ensure that these technologies are used in

a responsible and ethical manner, taking into account their potential

impact on human health, animal welfare, and the environment. New

technologies are transforming the food systems in various ways, from

improving efficiency in production and distribution to providing more

information to consumers about the food they eat. New technologies

are transforming the food system and creating new opportunities for

sustainable and equitable food production, distribution, and

consumption. However, it is important to ensure that these

technologies are developed and used in a responsible and ethical way

that benefits everyone in the food system.

Conclusion

The future of food systems will be shaped by a variety of factors,

including advances in technology, changes in consumer behaviour, and

global challenges such as climate change and food insecurity. The

future of food systems is likely to be shaped by a variety of factors,

including technological innovations, changing consumer preferences,

and global trends. Here are some potential trends and developments

that could shape the future of food systems,

Sustainable production

There is increasing pressure on food systems to become more

sustainable, with a focus on reducing greenhouse gas emissions,

conserving resources, and minimizing waste. This may involve the use

of new technologies such as precision agriculture, vertical farming, and cellular agriculture. As concerns about climate change and resource depletion continue to grow, there is likely to be an increasing emphasis on sustainable food systems. This could involve reducing waste, adopting regenerative agriculture practices, and incorporating alternative protein sources, among other strategies.

Plant-based and alternative proteins

There is growing demand for plant-based and alternative proteins as consumers seek more sustainable and healthy food options. This trend is driving innovation in areas such as plant-based meat substitutes and lab-grown meat. As demand for meat continues to grow, there is likely to be an increasing emphasis on alternative protein sources, such as plant-based and cultured meat. These products have the potential to reduce the environmental impact of food production and improve animal welfare.

Digitalisation

Digital technologies are transforming all aspects of food systems, from

farm to table. This includes the use of AI, blockchain, and the Internet

of Things to improve efficiency, traceability, and food safety.

Advancements in technology, such as robotics, AI, and precision

agriculture, are likely to continue to shape food systems in the future.

These technologies have the potential to improve efficiency, reduce

waste, and increase food safety

Personalised nutrition

As our understanding of nutrition and genetics continues to evolve,

there is likely to be an increasing emphasis on personalized nutrition.

This could involve using AI and other technologies to provide tailored nutrition recommendations based on an individual's health and dietary

preferences.

Circular economy

The circular economy approach involves designing food systems to

minimize waste and promote the reuse and recycling of materials. This

may involve new business models, such as food-sharing platforms, and

the development of new technologies for food waste reduction and

recycling.

Food security

Ensuring global food security will be a major challenge in the coming

years, particularly in the face of climate change and other

environmental pressures. This will require a focus on improving agricultural productivity, increasing access to nutritious food, and

reducing food waste.

Urban agriculture

As more people move to cities, there is likely to be an increasing

emphasis on urban agriculture, including rooftop gardens and indoor

farming. These practices have the potential to improve food security,

reduce food miles, and increase access to fresh produce.

The future of food systems will require innovative solutions that

balance environmental sustainability, economic viability, and social

equity. It will also require collaboration between all stakeholders,

including farmers, food producers, policymakers, and consumers. In

conclusion, innovative food systems are essential for creating a more sustainable and equitable food system that can meet the needs of a

growing global population while reducing environmental impact.

Innovative food systems are essential for creating a more sustainable,

equitable, and resilient food system that can meet the needs of a

growing global population. New technologies are revolutionizing the

food system, making it more efficient, sustainable, and resilient. the

future of food systems is likely to be shaped by a variety of factors,

including sustainability, technology, and changing consumer

preferences. It will be important to ensure that these developments

support the well-being of workers, consumers, and the environment.

By harnessing the power of these technologies, we can create a more

equitable and just food system that benefits all people and the planet.

New technologies are helping to transform food systems by improving

efficiency, transparency, and sustainability. New technologies are playing an increasingly important role in the food system, from the

farm to the table. However, it's important to ensure that these

technologies are used in a responsible and ethical way, with

consideration given to the potential social and environmental impacts.